3 9082 13008 7268

D1237752

The Bears Upstairs

A book of creative dramatics

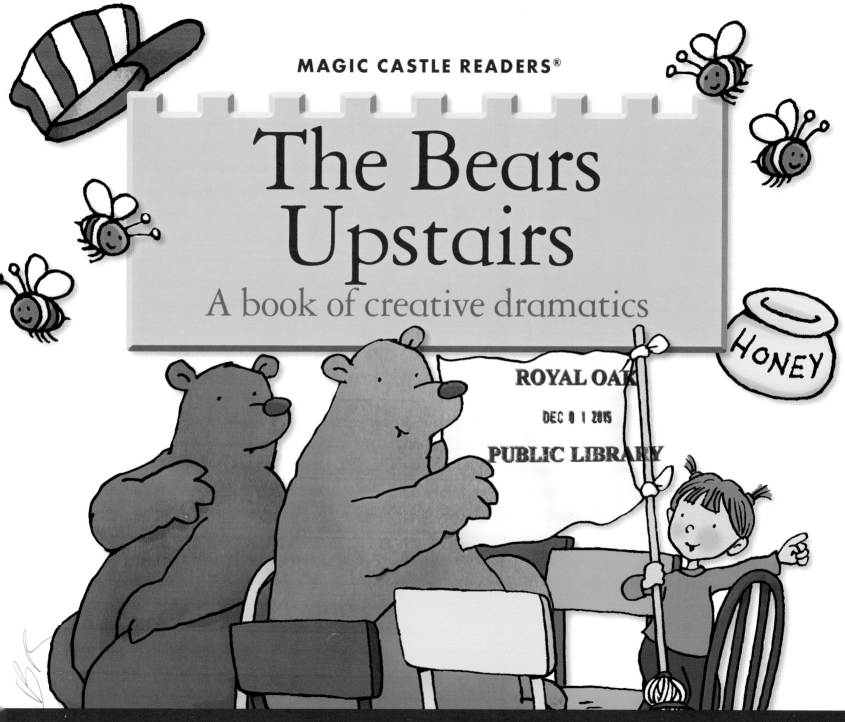

HONEY

BY JANE BELK MONCURE • ILLUSTRATED BY PATRICK GIROUARD

The Child's World®

Published by The Child's World®
1980 Lookout Drive • Mankato, MN 56003-1705
800-599-READ • www.childsworld.com

Acknowledgments
The Child's World®: Mary Berendes, Publishing Director
The Design Lab: Design
Jody Jensen Shaffer: Editing

ISBN 9781623235642
LCCN 2013931409

Printed in the United States of America
Mankato, MN
July 2013
PA02177

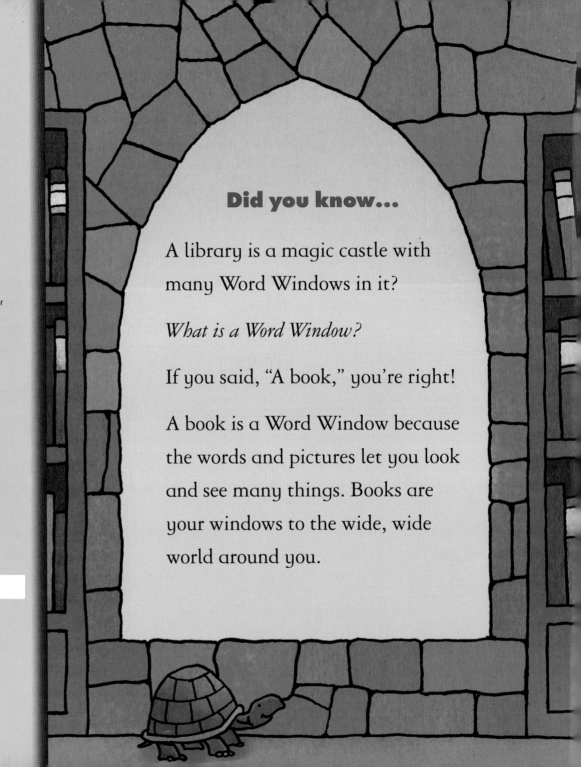

Did you know...

A library is a magic castle with many Word Windows in it?

What is a Word Window?

If you said, "A book," you're right!

A book is a Word Window because the words and pictures let you look and see many things. Books are your windows to the wide, wide world around you.

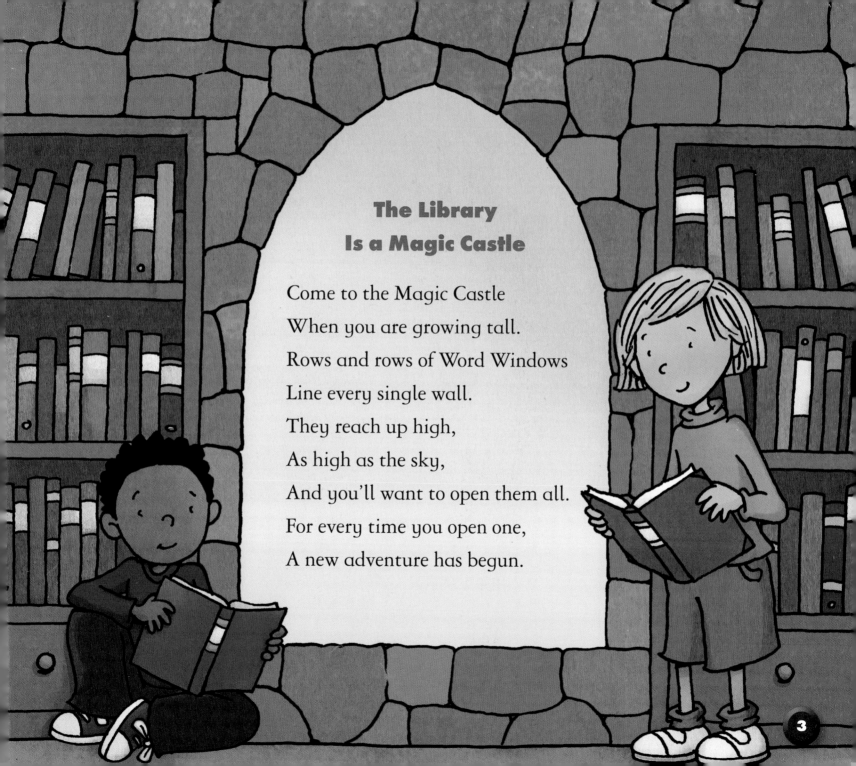

The Library
Is a Magic Castle

Come to the Magic Castle
When you are growing tall.
Rows and rows of Word Windows
Line every single wall.
They reach up high,
As high as the sky,
And you'll want to open them all.
For every time you open one,
A new adventure has begun.

Kate opens a Word Window.
Guess what she sees.

Kate sees stairs. Lots of stairs.

"I will go upstairs," she says.
Guess what Kate finds upstairs.

Kate finds bears. Lots of bears.

"Come and play," say the bears.

So Kate finds chairs. Lots of chairs.

"I will make something for the bears," Kate says.
She makes a boat out of chairs for the bears.

"Let's sail away," say the bears.

The bears make the chairs go up and down.
"We like to float in a chair boat," they say.

Then one bear asks,
"What else can we play today?"

"I know," says Kate.
She makes an airplane out of chairs for the bears.

"Let's fly high in the air," says a bear.
Away they go.

"What else can we play today?" ask the bears.

"Make a long line with your chairs," says Kate.

"Now we have a train.
Here we go, down the track.

All the way to town and back. TOOT! TOOT!
Here we go. Fast. Slow. Stop."

"What else can we play with our chairs?"
ask the bears.

Kate makes a bus out of chairs for the bears.
The bears sing a song as they bump along.

They bump up and down. The bears bump right out of their chairs and tumble to the floor.

"Oh my poor bears," says Kate.

Kate makes a hospital out of chairs for the bears.

Kate takes care of each bear.
"Don't cry," she says.

Kate goes downstairs.
She finds pears for the bears.

She shares the pears with the bears.

Then Kate makes a bed out of chairs for the bears.

She hugs each bear and says, "Good night."

Then Kate tiptoes down the stairs.

Kate closes the Word Window.
"I'll be back someday to play with
my bears upstairs," she says.

Questions and Activities

(Write your answers on a sheet of paper.)

1. Where does this story happen?
   Name two important things about that place.

2. Did this story have any words you don't know?
   How can you find out what they mean?

3. Who is the main character in this story?
   Write two things about her.

4. Name three ways the author tells the story.
   Name two things the author does to tell the story.

5. What does it mean when Kate says she'll be back someday to play with the bears upstairs? How do you know she means that?